Instructions for My Imposter

Also by Kathleen McGookey

Whatever Shines
(Marie Alexander Poetry Series)

We'll See: Poems by Georges L. Godeau (translation)

October Again (chapbook)

Mended (chapbook)

Stay
(A Tom Lombardo Poetry Selection)

Heart in a Jar

Nineteen Letters (chapbook)

Instructions *for* My Imposter

prose poems

Kathleen McGookey

Press 53
Winston-Salem

Press 53, LLC
PO Box 30314
Winston-Salem, NC 27130

First Edition

A Tom Lombardo Poetry Selection

Cover design by Claire V. Foxx

Cover art, "Horizon to Horizon," Copyright © 2015
by Dawn D. Surratt
instagram.com/ddhanna

Author photo by Kaitlin LaMoine Martin

Library of Congress Control Number
2019943434

Printed on acid-free paper
ISBN 978-1-950413-11-9

For Charlie and Lucy
I could not have written these poems without you

The author wishes to gratefully acknowledge the editors and staff of the periodicals where the following poems originally appeared, sometimes in different versions.

Alchemy: An Artists + Writers Initiative, "Appendix to Volume 11"
The American Journal of Poetry, "Instructions for My Imposter," "Short Catalog of My Regrets"
Arts and Letters, "In Paris"
Barn Owl Review, "Head Count"
Chicago Quarterly Review, "Gratitude Practice," "Here," "Ultrasound at Fifty"
Cloudbank, "Ordinary in the Light," "Three Days before My Birthday"
Columbia Poetry Review, "Late Summer Prayer," "Story for Combing Out Lice," "Epilogue, Spring"
Copper Nickel, "The Haunting," "The School of Anguish"
december, "Let Me Be as Patient as That Missing Pet Tortoise," "February Thaw," "Little Parenting Assignment #112"
Diode, "Change Your Life Through the Power of Math," "Into the Throat of Morning"
ELJ, "Letter to My Mother"
elsewhere, "Triage"
Field, "Star-Crossed"
Flash Flash Click, "Metaphor"
Glassworks/Flash Glass, "Whereas," "The Girl in the Feather Skirt Sends a Postcard"
Flash Glass, "She Steers Toward the Horizon"
KYSO Flash, "Feather Child," "Boy Meets Girl," "Taxonomy," "You Can Find Joy in Doing Laundry," "On a Scale of Zero to Ten," "Softball-Sized Eyeball Washes Up on Florida Beach," "At the Secretary of State," "That Couple with Their Heads Full of Clouds," "The Waiting"
Mid-American Review, "Spelling Lesson"
Miramar, "Red Phone Booth," "People Come and Go So Quickly Here"
One, "Luck," "I Have Forgotten Dusk"
Quarter After Eight, "Hearing Voices," "Such Pretty Fish"
Quiddity, "Living Inside the Sunrise," "The Skunk," "House Made of Words," "Message on a Star-Shaped Balloon"
Rattle, "At the Playground"
The Southern Review, "Fried Egg on a Plate without the Plate," "Solstice at Gun Lake"
Sweet, "Contradiction," "Someone Is Always Missing"
32 Poems, "Another Lullaby"
Tinderbox Poetry Journal, "I Could Promise to Try"
Tupelo Quarterly, "Invitation," "X-Ray"
Wake, "21 Things to Do with Envy"

"Metaphor" also appeared as a limited-edition broadside, with stunning art by Elizabeth King, through *Alchemy: An Artists + Writers Initiative*.

"Death, I Am Not in the Pamphlet" appears in my chapbook *Nineteen Letters*, published by BatCat Press.

"You Can Find Joy in Doing Laundry" was reprinted in *Best Microfiction 2019*.

"Boy Meets Girl" was reprinted in *Best Small Fictions 2019*.

"Late Summer Prayer," "Living Inside the Sunrise," and "That Couple with Their Heads Full of Clouds" appear as part of a longer piece in *Elemental: A Collection of Michigan Creative Nonfiction* (Wayne State, 2018).

Filmmaker Bryce Ury created a gorgeous short film of "Living Inside the Sunrise" for the Visible Poetry Project, which was released on April 13, 2019.

Contents

Invitation

Please come down and live with us. My daughter wants a simple playmate. My son wants help with his math. You will have to try one bite of roasted squash at dinner, but then we will give you the easiest chores: meal planning and sweeping up crumbs. If, that first night, you are homesick for sky, my daughter will comb your hair. We will not eat you or wash you or spend you or exhaust you. Then you can lift the sadness from what I've touched. We will not make you scrub your luminous footprints. We will not speak of those who are missing or the anger that rises up in me each night. We will let you sleep.

Let Me Be as Patient as That Missing Pet Tortoise

who survived thirty years in a locked attic, while underneath her the children washed and dried dishes, slapped each other, and grew. Someone sautéed onions, then stirred them into vegetable soup. The fresh wet smell of cut mango rose up. Let me praise the dim light from the dirty window under the eave, enough to nudge a path between the cracked television and knobless radio, then past a ripped footstool with stuffing blooming through its springs. Let me be as resilient: the vet guessed that tortoise ate termites from rotting upholstery and licked rainwater that streaked the walls. Let me forgive the lock and key, and my family who searched only the fenced garden, even after they discovered the open gate. Let me enter the lives of others by listening: a spoon circling in a teacup, a dropped key ring, a wren singing in the yard, and footsteps, quick and light. Let me praise hunger, one measure that I am alive.

The Skunk

Sometime in the night, that skunk you wanted to trap dug up the bees' nest and scattered papery combs around a hole the size of a large O—*oh, not you again*. It ate every bee, like delicate pale radish slices sprinkled with salt. The crisp tang. The unexpected struggle and crunch. Outside the doorway of our sleep. Outside the strip of orange light shimmering on our silence, that silence like a thread pulled from a bobbin, then wrapped around and around the house.

I Could Promise to Try

The dead always watched from their front row seats, lemon slices drifting in their cool drinks. They'd set down their binoculars and wipe their foreheads, pink air pressing around them like cotton candy. One would say, *This weather smells like blood* and the rest nodded, crossed their legs, and picked up their paper fans. Not one of those dead was a stranger to me. Some days I felt them in the baby's room among wallpaper clouds, watching him sleep. Some days I felt only their eyes as I buckled that squirming thing into his carseat: if I could just drive somewhere, I might accomplish something. With them watching me when the baby wailed, inconsolable, I could set him back in his crib and walk away.

Letter to My Mother

Sometimes I forget you for days. I pack sandwiches in brown bags and iron patches on jeans. I wash dishes, steam rising in my kitchen that smells like bread. When I walk through the early-morning fog, maybe I'll arrive where you are. Yesterday, my vision blurred as highway miles clicked by. I had only imagined your hand poised to stroke my forehead as I slept. Each day I wake, unsurprised at your absence. It is the gray sweater, soft as a rabbit, I pull on against the chill. It is the field outside my window, lush with bright clover that ripples in the wind. Soon, the farmer will harvest it so he can plant his fields in spring.

February Thaw

All winter, my daughter watched the broken branch in the catalpa print its upside down V on the sky. She stopped waiting for it to fall. Today, frost coats the brittle grasses in the field. They sway like the chatter of grackles when a flock lands at the feeder, all at once. We have only a little snow. Even what I thought was a hawk is just a clump of brown leaves. Both times I was pregnant, I never said, *Finally my body contains two hearts*. There were two of everything. It was the opposite of romance. Now, I can almost kiss her without bending as she writes *Fragile, Handle with Care* on a package she wants me to mail.

Feather Child

Daughter, how could we have known? They came without warning, silky, shiny, from swans and ducks, and covered you as you slept in your glass box. Your mouth disappeared. A fringe of down bloomed along your eyelashes and toes. I want to pet your sleek head, still turned away, and trace the pheasant feathers that trail down your back like a braid. And stroke your mottled soles. But any touch will trip the museum's alarm.

How can I stop watching this sleep?

You set out talismans on the windowsill—a pair of meadowlark's feet, a gray stone sprouting a plush tuft, a bit of driftwood shaped like a fox. All smaller than your thumb. Someone asks, *But where did they come from?* A sharpened white crayon. A needle, glistening.

Back home, our field of brambles and dead grasses is not quite covered in snow.

Whereas

The girl in the feather skirt gets tired of waiting for her story to start.
When would the mushroomy underside of the moon explode? *Darling,*
she writes, *I've sold your clothes.* She loves the slash and glister of her pen. *By
the time you read this, my ship will be en route.* Here on board, gold-tasseled
tablecloths sway. Petal by petal, an inchworm crosses the centerpiece of
lilies and phlox. The galley door swings, dishes clink, a kettle hisses.
Sometimes she strokes the cricket in her pocket for luck. Here on board,
staircases unfold into silken dark and tenderness begins at its regularly
scheduled time, nothing like a coin purse snapped closed. Snowflakes fall
like whispers and someone keeps shaking the globe.

Change Your Life Through the Power of Math

Translate your life into an equation and scribble it on a billboard—variables, parentheses, equals sign. Leave the answer blank. Reduce the ex-boyfriend in France to a square root, the builder who couldn't read blueprints to an imaginary number, your mother's missed diagnosis to the power of one. Math is comforting and reliable: change any figure to arrive at a different, more elegant solution. Such an equation is more valuable than a time machine, because even if you met your younger self stepping off a yellow bus or locking her grad school office, she wouldn't listen to the earnest, graying lady you've become.

Numbers clarify, like a microscope or a pair of binoculars. They don't lie. Put this billboard bearing the equation of your life somewhere near the World's Largest Truckstop on I-80, where the brown grass in the median sways. When night falls, your inscrutable numbers will blink in the headlights like constellations. One of those travelers might be the girl you once were, and to her, maybe the flash of the billboard is a door cracked open, a little light spilling through.

Boy Meets Girl

In a twinkling, the girl turns into a sparrow, the boy into a wren. No, girl into ocean waves churning, boy into froth, wind, sunlight glinting on shore. Or boy into rooster, girl into fox. Possibly a hunting party gathers. Possibly another suitor and maiden hide in the wood and watch the chase while the girl slowly combs her luxurious red hair. The boy and girl move like flames glimpsed from the corner of an eye. It might be mercy, that escape from such monstrous desire. But not as comets ablaze across the velvet night. No, not as moonlight resting lightly on any body of water. Maybe boy into lightning, girl into struck rock. Maybe girl into oak, boy into ivy, into moss, climbing up, trailing down. Does it matter?

Metaphor

A spotlight, flicked on. A globe full of air, suspended, no sloshing water, no fog. An onion, a turnip, a potato, peeled and ready for stew. A lost silver birthday balloon, rising in the sky. A charm made to hang from a sick girl's neck. A dirty snowball, rolled in the yard. A stainless colander next to the white mixing bowl. For heaven's sake, talk about something else. It doesn't care who gazes upon it, especially you, unschooled, or your onion-skin promises, ring box open.

Mornings after, it's a blood orange, sliced and dripping on the clouds. Make that tarnished silver dollar into a watch, and it just might love its own movement or the hands that stroke its face.

Into the Throat of Morning

Only the slender words swim this far.

My luck lives in a rice-paper house I keep on my bookshelf. She doesn't mind the dust. Her heart is a broken black cricket, wings slick as oil. Maybe today she will sing. I feed her what I catch—spiders, rose petals, a hawk feather or two—but she never says what she requires.

Taxonomy

Months later, when my husband finally scratched my bare back, the itchy center part I couldn't reach, tiny sugar ants streamed out, then carpenter ants and termites, crickets and earwigs and millipedes, then silverfish, furry disoriented bumblebees, a few fireflies, green grasshoppers, and moths with large eyes glaring from their wings. He leapt out of bed to scoop them into glass jars with metal lids and line them up on the headboard. The snakes settled into the bathtub, its candlelit waters still smelling of vanilla and blood orange, little waves lapping the sides. In Sharpie, he catalogued his find by genus and species on the back of his hand and forearm. I missed the electricity of all those wings inside my skin. *This will never teach him*, I thought.

The Haunting

They lived with the ghost of the old boyfriend who only appeared in mirrors and haunted the perimeters of rooms, glowering and pouting against the walls. He never said a word but watched her daughters eat dinner, carry their plates to the sink, and open their notebooks. He watched her practice stain removal in many forms. Their sweaters shrunk. They grew out their hair. Her daughters looked just like her. The new man wore flannel shirts and took care of sheep—unusual in this day and age, but he liked the outdoors. She called him in when smoke filled the house. The ghost unsettled visitors, whether they could see him or not. If asked about a chill or flicker, she'd say, *That's just David, my old boyfriend from Europe.* Sometimes he loitered at the window and let moonlight illuminate his face. Or he gazed into the foggy dawns, pretending to see an airplane glinting as it approached snow-capped mountains. His loyalty, though misplaced, had become a point of honor. In the early days, she ordered him to leave, burned juniper, and hung a wreath of blackberry and ivy on her door. They moved and moved again, and he always came along. She hardly ever wondered how to say *feather* or *cloud* in French. She guessed she was not the first person to live this way.

Hearing Voices

Once a witch caught a child and cut off an ear. She tossed it to her rats, who hissed and spit and clawed until one carried it away to eat. The next day, the ear emerged from the rat's back, pink and delicate and whole. From then on, the child heard everything. Some rats grew two human ears and discovered they worked like wings. When the children heard the wind's soft hum, they sighed, tucked their thumbs in their mouths and dreamed of the ocean. The witches were not pleased. They sent the rats to the undertaker's basement, the jail, the slaughterhouse. Soon the earless children thrashed in their damp beds. Their parents tried, a little, to comfort them. But they were tired. So the children rose early, gathered berries, swept the leaves off the walk. They built toy houses with white pebbles they found in their yards. Their hands shook.

House Made of Words

A light shone in the window of the little house made of words. In the bedroom, someone changed sheets. In the kitchen, someone flipped crepes. In the basement, mortar crumbled between fieldstones. No one had fallen down the stairs or smashed the back door window and reached in to turn the knob. No one had carried a choking infant into the yard, calling out for help. And help would come. But today, someone dangled a knife over the heating vent and down it slid with a metallic gasp, clicking and shuddering. Someone leaned an elbow on the windowsill while a bonfire leaped in the yard, tall as that second-story window, and scraps of ash rose on currents of air. Someone blew a kiss to the question marks. The house did not tremble in the night. Besides, it was only dusk, the kind of dusk filled with falling leaves and falling stars, dusk with its life still stretched out before it, a wide ribbon of honey tipped from the jar.

Tuesday Morning

I hemmed dress pants for the funeral and the skin on my knuckles cracked and bled. On his phone, he kept pictures of nests and eggs—phoebe, bluebird, wren. The children bent over the twiggy cups and counted each clutch: seven, three, five. *Always a prime number*, my daughter said. I don't want to be upset like this again. In silhouette, beetles glittered on her glow-in-the-dark terrarium. Amelia Bedelia always got out of a mess by baking something sweet. I set out a worn cotton T-shirt to put on, later.

Here

While she was waking up after emergency surgery, my mother blinked and said in a bright slurred voice, *Here I am!* Like she had just burst out from her hiding place. Then she closed her eyes. A few minutes later, she lifted her head and said it again. She didn't yet know what they had done to her body to keep it temporarily in this world. After she knew, she didn't complain. The visiting nurse didn't say the stoma looked like a rosebud. He taught us to look in our bathroom mirror and trace its shape on the adhesive of the colostomy bag. We tried our best but didn't always get it right. In the end, it hardly mattered.

After the Thunderstorm, April

Overhead, oaks unfurl a fringe of new leaves. Torn daffodils bow, trumpets closed, browning petals clumped like wet tissue. A ladybug crawls along my notebook's edge, then turns the corner, its six black legs thinner than commas. I still wish you could hear me. My scratched wristwatch tells only one kind of time, hour after hour. Out in the field, everything that begins is pulsing again. Nothing is making a list. That one sleek swallow could circle in front of the bleached clouds all day.

Message on a Star-Shaped Balloon

For months it hung tangled in the catalpa at the edge of our field. When the wind blew and the sun shone, it glittered. The children pointed and climbed as high as I would let them. By then the catalpa had shed its white mess. At night coyotes wailed. The trunk split, a ragged hollow torn in the upright half, and the balloon slipped free. The children chased it, caught it, smoothed the crumpled message: *God, I have no one. I'm sorry. I'm sorry. I'm sorry.* The last of the rain dripped from the wide leaves and wet our shoulders. A flock of wild turkeys walked like shadows through the shining field.

The next day, my son folded his reply into a wad and left it in the catalpa's splintered heart. My daughter ripped hers to bits, then scattered them from the lowest limbs.

Nostalgia

The summer I turned ten, Japanese beetles piled their iridescent, green-black bodies into the open faces of the moss roses, then pushed their prickly legs over each other to reach the fringed yellow centers. They weren't real roses, not the red romantic kind, one dozen declarations of love. Planted out back on the property line, they smelled like the pink soap in my fussy aunt's bathroom. If I could ask my mom, she'd know their Latin name. *What imagined sweetness were those beetles gorging on?* I wondered, still young enough to want to play catch with my dad, tossing a baseball back and forth, into the dusky, thickening air.

Red Phone Booth

at the edge of a pine forest. Black rotary phone, disconnected; I lift the receiver to my ear:

Like the pearly rush inside a seashell. Like a twig tapping glass, hope's brief flare. Like absent static. Like the foggy echo of my pulse.

Do you think of me—I've got gray hair now—little stick figure waving in your ghost telescope: *Here I am, hello, I'm still here—*

People Come and Go So Quickly Here

A little red house swooped and hovered overhead, then landed on a patch of plush grass. Daisies and lilacs and a picket fence sprang up. My children raced through the yard and my mother followed from the front door, carrying a tray of iced lemonade. With each step, the tall glasses trembled and chimed. I had forgotten she was dead and I hugged her, two separate times, while cherry blossoms drifted like snow around us. We didn't shiver. It had been so long. She'd come back, she said, because she needed a phone book. She wanted to look someone up. I forgot to grab the children and say, *Here's the granny I've told you so much about.*

Fried Egg on a Plate without the Plate

is something my daughter might order, rumpled with sleep. She is bigger
now. She stretches like a cat when I stroke her arm and her white headboard
wobbles. Last night she left me weeds with starry blooms and feathery stalks,
a purple bow tied to the vase. I give her cinnamon toast, broiled in the oven.
She says, *I don't want that*. She plays "Ode to Joy" shrill and too fast on her
brown plastic recorder, then stops, inhales, and does it again.

X-Ray

Skeletons ride the bus to class or work or the flower shop to buy a lavender bouquet. One reads the paper standing up. When they exit, they gather their briefcases and umbrellas and hats. See the nickels in their pockets, the matchstick carrots in their lunches? The St. Christopher medal dangling from the teddy bear's neck? The little skeletons like to sit in back.

At the office, skeletons take the elevator rather than the stairs. Here are levers and cogs, perfectly aligned, a steel rope snaking through skull-shaped wheels bolted to the metal box. Elsewhere, skeletons shake hands by the water cooler or peer into the depths of the copy machine. They pin paper squares on a bulletin board, then rearrange them. The light in the room comes from their bones.

Contradiction

No, not every story is about the body. Take this one: my father dies. The sky and earth, even the field corn in unwavering rows, close neatly around that unoccupied space.

I held the slight weight of absence in my palm before I scattered it under the wild dogwood, then brushed ash from my fingertips. The trees were blooming lavishly that year.

Late Summer Prayer

Let spiders nest in my daughter's paper lanterns, hung from the porch for her slumber party. Let fireflies and moths light the extravagant dark, thick with biting insects doing their work. Let those with broken wings find someone determined, armed with scissors and tweezers and glue. When the storm sweeps across the lake, all wind and hard rain, let rain and lake boil in a frenzy of spray. Let rotting peaches bury their dull buzzing back underground. Let the toddler dressed as an owlet escape her flimsy cage. A real owl perches on the zookeeper's arm, right out of a book. And because we leave the bookstore at midnight, let the yellow animal eyes of traffic lights blink us all the way home. The next morning, if a fledgling robin flies straight into our window, let it die quickly, its spotted chest pearly as twilight on the grass. Now we can get as close as we want.

Ultrasound at Fifty

Cut basil sprouts skeleton tendrils in a glass next to my sink. I just meant to save it for a day. I forgot that quiet, hidden force, wetly propagating. I forgot the ultrasound's underwater whoosh, valves ticking, spark of news, buzz-whir-click. Only my heartbeat this time. In the waiting room, I type my name into a computer and a woman says, *You're in the right place.* The technician checks the pulse behind my knee, then slides the wand over the teensy grief, size of a kidney bean, that sprang up overnight in my thigh. She doesn't invite me to view the screen.

Luck

Do you remember when a flock of grackles landed in the yard at Miner Lake and caught us inside its black chatter, everywhere shining feathers, shining beaks, everywhere grackles pecking the grass with little jerky motions, swarming the sidewalk and the picnic table, flashing their flat wet eyes as if we were shrubs or flagpoles, the sky gray and white and ribbed like muscles, and even though we froze, breath held, wide-eyed, they startled up again, flew as one body to the neighbor's catalpa, left us ordinary, laughing, dazed, and I said, *I'll get groceries if you'll make dinner.*

Someone Is Always Missing

Like that red fox, black-tipped tail long as its body, flashing across the dirt
road, I might believe you have just stepped away from your desk—

Unknown caller, my phone blinks, and I answer anyway. *Hello?*
Hello? I repeat, into the open line—

Star-Crossed

While I slept, Death pinned up linen swatches in my brain. Then he knocked out some walls. New curtains can only do so much. *What this place needs,* Death said, *is a little more light.* I blinked. I liked my furrowed dark and unraveling afghans, red onion in the pantry sending up shoots. It was cozy like a grandma's apartment over the funeral home, there by the freeway exit that was under construction for years. Death carried a clipboard with a shiny metal clamp. He ordered a Danish couch, all leather and chrome. What I wanted didn't matter. On his copy of the blueprint, he drew a dotted line where the skylight would go.

The Girl in the Feather Skirt Sends a Postcard

To Whom It May Concern: Today I plunged into the living room and the lovely bubbles of my breath rose through the crystal ropes of the chandelier. Sunlight on water makes waves like fish scales, iridescent even from underneath. The pale overstuffed couch swayed. Blurry shadows soared above the surface, calling each other with reedy, two-step notes. The windows are open but the water will not leave the house. That's one hidden rule. Here's another: inside my sleep I am never lonely. I've set out white teacups on the windowsill for us, a little trail of bones.

Triage

When her water balloon the size of a baby develops a leak, my daughter wraps it in a towel and lugs it inside, demanding tape. Then she sets up a hospital under the patio umbrella. Band-aids over the criss-cross X don't stop the slow ooze, so she brushes on watercolors to strengthen its latex skin. She writes get-well notes from the patient's family and classmates, and twists a yellow pipe cleaner into a heart. A blue-and-orange butterfly lands and uncoils its tongue. My daughter refolds the stained towel in the water balloon's shoebox bed. The patient jiggles and lolls. After it collapses in a rush, she fills another with the hose, then carefully pierces its black neck.

Story for Combing Out Lice

Once an owl carried a pearl past twilight, past midnight, far past 3 a.m. It flew over the seashore and its billion grains of sand. It flew over forests and highways, airports and malls. The owl was just a speck in the sky. It solved a story problem to win the pearl. It beat up another owl and stole it from the nest. Really, the owl just liked the sound—*pearl*—and swam through five oceans to find one. Then it came looking for you. It flew and flew, hungry and mightily sick of the pearl, which sometimes gasped and sighed. And in its hunger, the owl forgot its task. Outside our bedroom window, it killed a skunk, the first thing it saw. An awful stink seeped into our dreams: a child slept on a pillow bristling with pins. You missed the bus and arrived at school wearing only a towel. The pearl, bigger than a nit but smaller than a pea, sank right down in the grass. Scared of heights and chilled, so far from home, the pearl thought, *Maybe this is a new kind of ocean.* Crisp outlines of cornstalks emerged in the dawn. You'd need a searchlight, a flashlight, a lighted microscope to see the pearl blink and shiver in that wave of green.

Living Inside the Sunrise

I will build us a glass boat to drift on apricot currents of light. I will pack blankets and a thermos of sweet milk. Here, inside the day's flush, we begin and begin, our plans suspended like dewdrops: plant a sunflower seed, write a note in purple marker, help a box turtle cross the road. You might lean against me and stroke my hair. If the weather changes, we'll pull on yellow slickers and hats, and say the gray clouds feel soft as fur. If the sun rises over a farm, we'll look down on goldfinches flickering through the cornfield. If the sun rises over a lake, calm as a cat's clear eye, our other, watery selves will wave up at us.

Little Parenting Assignment #112

At breakfast, don't tell your daughter you dreamed she was eaten by a bear. Mute, shocked awake, you counted ordinary dangers—gymnastic coaches, drunks, someday walking alone across campus at night, malfunctioning cans of mace. Instead, say, *Don't the clouds look like whipped cream? Sweetened with cinnamon and honey?* Put some on her waffle, along with sliced pears. Kiss her as she leaves for the bus stop and inhale. She smells like bubblegum lip gloss. Her footprints through the frosted grass vanish down the hill. Even though the day opens gray and beige, the sky lightens with the sheen from spilled gasoline. The bare oaks stand black and upright, waiting for spring.

You Can Find Joy in Doing Laundry

Laundry is loyal. Laundry always waits, unlike a hungry friend or a French lover. Laundry needs you like a floor needs a mop. It's not just work, it's joy, available for the taking. Nothing smells like a fresh start like a load of whites, tossed in at 3 a.m. after a child threw up, a woeful stuffed lamb tumbling dizzily among the sheets. If bleach doesn't work, try baking soda. Try Cascade mixed with a half cup of Dawn. Remember to blot and never scrub. Blood, chocolate, and Elmer's glue usually never leave you, constant as weather, but other stains grow pale, then drift off like ghosts to gaze at the clouds. And though their presence bothered you at first, you forget them so easily, like stray thoughts, like that boy who smelled of mint and his mother's detergent sitting next to you in tenth-grade biology, who held your hand at the movies, once. He had black hair and long eyelashes and fingernails bitten to the quick. What was his name?

Instructions for My Imposter

Do not burn bridges with the school secretaries or the librarian who lets you use her copy machine. You'd drown in a minute if they didn't keep the boy's migraine pills in a drawer, unauthorized. At home, you'll need sharpened pencils, dollar bills, and a place to store permission slips. People call and hang up all day long. When stillness fills the house, scrub honey off the counter, sweep sugar off the floor, and glue the yellow gauze butterfly back together. After school, the girl drops it in the Goodwill bin. Almost everyone will speak to you from the living room while you wash dishes. Don't try to sleep when you're mad. Instead, spread peanut butter on bread, wait for sunrise's blurred silk, and make a list of what you'll accomplish today. At the top, write, *Forget about time*. It doesn't care one bit about you, while three kinds of blue—wind, water, sky—rush past.

Short Catalog of My Regrets

Regret Number 12 reads over my shoulder. My fourth regret follows me from room to room, then scratches its ear, collar jingling. Sixteenth regret leans against any available wall, torn jeans and messy hair. Regret 7 tells me now it has heard everything. Thirty-eighth regret washes my face with a warm, soapy cloth. They take turns sleeping. They juggle name tags and paper clips and count the stars. Regret 3 chews its scabby lips while my twenty-ninth regret vacuums the stairs. Regrets 131 and 8 play a wicked game of hopscotch in the kitchen. Yesterday's regret roosts in my head and preens its oily wings.

21 Things to Do with Envy

Buy it a one-way ticket to Iceland; sew it a black velvet cape; tape its mouth shut and shave its head; give it a motorcycle but no helmet, a hockey stick, a chainsaw; tell it, *You're nothing without me*; send it to sleep with Whitman and plant sunflowers in the dug-up earth that smells like worms and rot; make it wear bifocals; hand it a sparkler; look it in the eye—don't look away first; teach it to pray; teach it to say *pretty please*; boil it with the blackberry jam, then watch it glisten in the pantry all winter; slice it and throw it to the bass; pour it down the kitchen sink, follow with baking soda, vinegar, and a whole teakettle of boiling water; slip it a bottle of sleeping pills; drop it down the sewer, the hospital elevator shaft, off the Sixth Street Bridge; give it a warm bath, graham crackers and milk, and beg it to stay in its own bed tonight; lose it on a field trip to the zoo; heap its plate with bacon again and again and again; pack it with ceramic pumpkins and witch's feet, then tell Envy if it's very, very good, you might let it out once a year.

Head Count

I walked in on my roommate changing her head, cuddling the one she'd just removed against her shoulder. She was stroking its brown ringlets. As she set it in its duffel bag, the head said my roommate had changed me, too, while I slept: now I was a sweet and dimwitted gas station clerk from Ohio. I felt same as always, but the head offered a torn picture of my new mother. And my husband in our bedroom? A youthful head from a science teacher in Idaho on a newly slim and hairless body. I opened the door to check. Someone waggled his fingers at me from bed. *I want his correct head on his correct body*, I told my roommate. *I'm going to count to five.* I really said that—correct head, correct body. She rummaged in the supply closet for a minute, rearranged vials, shook out a few pillowcases, but nothing turned up. That's what she said. And my husband—if you could call it that—just wanted me to lie down.

The School of Anguish

Scarred wooden desks line up in rows. Miss Valenetti wears red heels and a clingy yellow dress. We may not say she looks like a volcano or sunset or fishing lure. Instead of doing our spelling lesson, she tells us last night's dream: she dove through a hole in the ice to retrieve matches chained to a cinder block. She couldn't open the box. We may not say our dreams or ask questions about that stubborn box. In gym class, we sit in a circle while Mr. Tully unties our shoes and cries. Then he ties them again. We don't even play duck-duck-goose. At lunchtime, the cafeteria ladies scoop boiled tongue onto our blank trays.

Such Pretty Fish

Once a witch caught another child for the goldfish bowl on her mantle. She named it Hansel-or-Gretel and popped it right in. At first, swimming was like flying over the playground, silky red-gold kite-fins trailing. But of course, the children could speak to one another. They searched under the slimy bridge for a hidden door. Through the bowl's clear curves, the kitchen pans showed only their moon faces. The water grew cold. Meanwhile, the witch practiced: goldfish into crab into rock back into gasping, dog-paddling child. By then, night had fallen. The children tried to tread water but their chins slipped under. Candles projected halos onto the water as the children floated on their backs, beautiful and tragic like nineteenth-century paintings. Finally, the children called in tinny voices, *Come in! The water's fine!* And the witch paused. She didn't receive many invitations. Such talented pets! Such pretty experiments! But she liked them best as bright fish, with large mouths and wide eyes. When they cried, she wouldn't know.

Spelling Lesson

When a vagabond butterfly enters the classroom, the children erase it. They are good students, troubled by shadowy wings underneath their spelling list: persimmon, bittersweet, nest, paw. When a bluebird follows, the children erase until bits of feather drift in the air. They want to please their teacher, who writes in red on a white board up front. Outside, a red-tailed hawk lands on the scarecrow's pitchfork handle. No one asks to use the bathroom. The hawk sits absolute inside the classroom's held breath. The children don't blink.

On a Scale of Zero to Ten

My pain dragged me, hunched and limping, past the nurse who searched for my test results, past the double metal doors that swung open like gates to a glistening country, then into and out of a white room with blue sky taped to the ceiling. Like a gathering wave made of sand, my pain grew so steadily it seemed to have always existed, darkly immobile, inside me. My pain closed down the ER, got shuttled to the orange hallway, then the blue hallway, where they parked my bed against a wall and gave my husband a plastic chair. We tried not to eavesdrop on pain that didn't belong to us, hidden behind curtains. It was the deepest part of night. Our children had put themselves to bed, we hoped, and now slept like stones or birds or rain. To show I was a good sport, I tried to vomit quietly. The surgeon who leaned over me refused to state the worst case I might wake to. He wore a flawless shirt, cream-colored silk, but one tip of his collar was tucked under itself. In another scenario, I might have reached out to fix it.

You Have Nothing to Be Afraid of, Anymore—

Not even silver tanker trucks hauling liquid manure up and down the dirt road in regular rotation, spreading dust and stink through the air, or cancer growing lush and unbridled in your pancreas though you've always felt just fine, or the silvery seductive gaze of the phone in your son's palm, better than a lover because he can tickle it awake anytime, or the broken branch that has dangled for months in the crook of the aspen, above the flower bed where the bearded irises are just beginning to stir, it's spring after all and someone has to pull weeds. There's time, you think, there must be time because it's spring and the swallows are singing though it's already midday, there's time to crumple a chocolate wrapper and offer it like fool's gold to the trash collectors, time to close your eyes while a nurse draws your blood into a labeled vial, your ears ringing, enough time to blow an eyelash from your fingertip—but under these circumstances, what would a wish matter?

Death, I Am Not in the Pamphlet

you just shoved in your pocket, so don't bother checking pages 3 or 7, or
even the back, all of which are blissfully blank. If you care to, write my
history while I try again to wash the rust from my hair. Be sure to mention
that whenever anyone says odalisque, I dash off to look it up. That my
imaginary barn is missing a good chunk of roof and so cannot hold the
owls who come each spring, calling for mates. That the owls are not like a
coalition of shadows. That furthermore, I am ashamed we bulldozed and
dug and poured cement in the midst of their perfectly good forest. No
animal lately has breathed on my forehead. See?

Softball-Sized Eyeball Washes Up on Florida Beach

A clear, deep blue, the eyeball was darkest in its center—picture an abyss—and ringed in black. The scientists took turns cradling it in their gloved hands. When night settled over the laboratory, they held it to the window and showed it the moon. Then the scientists flung themselves into their gold-filigreed thrones, deeply dismayed. The moon and the eyeball had ignored each other. The scientists wrapped and unwrapped the eyeball in silver heat-reflecting blankets. They tested it for loneliness and ghosts. They weighed it in ounces and grams and calculated its equivalent in vapor. Not all scientists approved of this approach. At the water cooler, a small group grumbled. *If someone has something to say*, one scientist said in a high, tight voice, *I wish she'd just say it.* That scientist clicked her pen and clipped it onto her white pocket. Anyone could see this wasn't a friendly eyeball, yet they still petted its back, where a few stringy muscles dangled, so as not to obscure its view. They rolled it through the maze reserved for rats and recorded its speed. No one was surprised when the eyeball couldn't find its way back to the start. Every test proved inconclusive. In the end, the scientists settled for sitting in a circle and gazing into its blue-black depths. Even though it felt like drowning, none could look away.

She Steers Toward the Horizon

The girl in the feather skirt opens door Number 2. Behind door Number 1 are rain and hail, tornadoes, a roiling mess. Door Number 3 conceals a hearse. She doesn't mind silence, so she drives around her island. She just got her learner's permit. It's slow going, but she likes the wind on her skin, how the hearse gleams like polished leather, even the steep hills with no barriers between herself and the sea. Alone on the road, the girl tightens her seatbelt as kitchen windows blink past: a woman peels carrots: a man sharpens knives. A dog howls behind a picket fence. The girl in the feather skirt never thinks about the other doors. She hums. A door is not the story of a bright blue sky. She memorizes fractions and their decimal equivalents. She pets her skirt which she wears like an invisible shield. Like an opal, its color changes by increments, depending on the light.

In Paris

Back when my hair did not smell of burning leaves, when each day unfurled its lonely petals like frost etching a train window, when my stomach was flat and I contained only contradictory selves, I followed you to a grocer on the Champs Elysees and bought two green apples, one for now, one for later. I could have been anyone with all the time in the world. I followed you through doors of bone I did not understand were doors while water dripped and echoed. My heart knocked to be let back in. Back then, my grief was a rabbit in a shoebox. My regret was an egg. My anger grew mums that bloomed like blue flames. You were a carpet of feathers, a flock of swans, migrating, and every radiant mirror.

Ordinary in the Light

Speaking of loss, here's another sunrise with snowflakes drifting in crisp air like pure decoration. An hour later, the pampas grass has shaken off its white tassels. A trail of footprints leads behind the garage. In art class, my daughter cuts out a small black figure, pastes it on crayoned waves, and writes, *Icarus is swimming with a swan.*

I can't say what my language makes. Not a windswept shore, spray drenching the pier. Not a blue city. Maybe a tea party, with three-legged stools and chipped dishes. Inside a thin cloud that surely won't hold us, that might send down snow.

Procedure

My ghosts fold green oak leaves into bowls, then float them, full of marigolds and lit candles, down the river. They stay busy. I slip out, fairly empty, fairly sure I could never feel hungry again—

When the nurse leaves, her hurry-web swirls the curtain. My gurney faces the window. My husband does not see me wipe my cheek with my thumb—

My ghosts peer into a cement leaf cast from a real one, rhubarb, open like a palm to the sky, and fill that cup-shaped hollow with rain and a little mold—

My mother. My mother had cancer. My mother died, I say to the nurse, the intern, the slight doctor with white hair who bends over me—

How could time behave? It does not speak my language.

Three Days before My Birthday

Fog blurs the trees at the edge of my field, so I can't see the farmhouse next door, or the road beyond, or the water tower watching over three elementary schools with their locked lobbies. The air is a damp blanket pulled up to my cheeks. Easy enough to imagine living in a cloud, our minds dulled by driving hundreds of highway miles. Someone might bring us plates of waffles or take out Chinese. No one would make promises. This morning, the bathroom mirror fell out of its frame but didn't break.

At the Playground

A boy on a bicycle tried to outrun a witch, but the witch snagged his shadow with her teeth and reeled him in. *I'm only ten*, the boy said. *And you will be delicious*, the witch replied. She stroked his hand with both thumbs. She kissed his palm, then broke off his pinky and swallowed. *Delicious*, she repeated, and gingerbread crumbs stuck to the gummy corners of her mouth. The boy could not believe his body would act like that. He felt like a birthday cake missing its candles. So he offered her a flat dead snake from his pocket. *But I've left my heart at home.* And he could see it, safe in a glass jar, pulsing, next to his fish tank. The witch was crestfallen and tried not to show it. *A science project?* she said, and opened her black umbrella. The next gust blew her high into the air. Her boots rattled against each other as she grew smaller and smaller. She was sorry to lose him. At least he had not spoiled her appetite.

Tinder

The boy had a castle and a match. Everyone was doing it. He struck the match in the round tower, looking out at the fields of the kingdom, the school buses idling in the parking lot. It wasn't his kingdom, exactly. He had snuck into the castle. He had stolen the match. What were his plans, exactly? The boy's heart was a dam, ready to burst. It had already been patched a remarkable number of times. The boy could have begun in the library or the cafeteria. But up here in the tower, he could hear his pulse, the slow jangle of keys on the custodian's belt. He could almost see the ocean laid out at the horizon, probably glittering. Of course a pile of dry hay nestled against the stone wall. A family of mice lived there. Meanwhile, his match flickered. In a few seconds, his fingers would burn.

Epilogue, Spring

I take waffles again to the family next door. Sometimes I leave them on the porch while their Great Dane barks. Sometimes my friend emerges, disheveled, and gathers the ripped brown bag I offer into her arms. This is how I say I am sorry, still, that her daughter killed herself last year. My friend stacks the plastic bags I have labeled and dated in the freezer in her cluttered garage. Sometimes we talk about her younger daughter. Who has just set a school record in backstroke. Who has brought home, for Mother's Day, a crumpled yellow pansy in a Dixie cup, ready for planting.

At the Secretary of State

The take-a-number machine hits 100 and rolls over. Four rows of chairs, all full. The spring afternoon carries on its business outside the window. From time to time, a person or couple gives up, rises, and lets a white slip drift to the floor like an apple blossom petal or cabbage butterfly. After the door clicks shut, the beige walls swallow each brief absence as if numbers 12 or 20 or 64 have never been there at all.

Solstice at Gun Lake

She casts her line but someone has removed the hook for safety. She sits at the end of the dock—not far, a little far—while a few adults watch from shore. She is not the littlest one but her feet don't touch the lake. A snake glides like a ribbon through the water. Just last week, a girl she knew stepped in front of a pickup truck. Then she found a crushed oriole, an orange-and-black pile by the road. What will happen next? Time stirs the clouds into eyes, into mouths, into dragons and valleys and fish scales. The dark is still coming. A family of swans preens in the shallows. They leave behind a scattering of feathers, unnecessary now, drifting like fragile toy boats.

That Couple with Their Heads Full of Clouds

is sailing on stirred-up August water, more green than any shade of blue. She reclines on the seat, a rolled-up towel under her neck. When the boat tilts, she grabs the edge. He's careful, usually, but wind's capricious— rippling or dying, flapping the rainbow-striped sail. She closes her eyes. She doesn't mention the child's spider bite, new shoes, new notebooks, new blank forms, the lemon cake she'd like to make. Instead, she imagines clear bubbles in the sailboat's wake, swirling before they dissolve. The water smacks its small mouths against the hull. They might hold hands, briefly, here inside the wind's rush and lull, until he pulls the mainline in. What happens next is out of their control. Sometimes an eagle flies overhead. Sometimes a gull.

I Have Forgotten Dusk

I have forgotten dusk and the hundred crows perched in the bare oak outside the hospital, angels buzzing in our ears like mosquitoes, the dark murmuring and settling in. I have also forgotten the moment, hours later, when darkness lifted, stars fading like roadside litter, gray field and gray sky emerging once again, the maidenhair grasses leaning under their tassels as if the light were too much to bear.

Another Lullaby

I'll hide a nightlight inside this word. Inside this one, a cracked bike helmet. Inside this, a just-scraped elbow, knuckle, forehead—take your pick—and its slow bloom of blood. And inside this, the weathered wooden swing set, its swings tossed high over the warped and mossy top bar. Sit with me and I'll plump up my pillows of worry into feathers and clouds, so cozy you'd swear you were safe in your own bed. What did I expect? As planned, the children learned to mop and slice sandwiches and drive. To leave footprints and tire tracks in the snow. Inside this last word, I'll tuck a jagged paper daisy that you can pin to your coat. Try it on. You'll be surprised how happy you'll feel.

Gratitude Practice

Thank you for the gray and fraying milkweed pods ready to release swirling clouds of silk, for the pumpkins, not yet rotten, for my children interrupting at mealtime, the greasy knife clattering to the floor, water pooling under our glasses; thank you for the thankless task of making dinner again, for the smudged and sticky kitchen floor, for the nights that come so early now, rain turned briefly to hail and back again; thank you for the phone call that the car went off the road but not into a tree; thank you for the chocolate cake though it's burned and I forgot the frosting, for the child who stood by my bed last night and whispered again and again until I jerked awake; thank you for eye rolling, for *I'll do it in a minute*, for *You wouldn't understand*, we have so little time together after all; thank you for my mother and father, absences we search for in the sky; thank you for the broken dishwasher, for the repairman who calls back but can't stop by today, and thank you for the yellow leaves shaped like teardrops drifting from the birch, which hover a little, then fall as if falling is all they'll ever do—

The Waiting

After a brief hard rain, a turkey vulture flew to our dead oak and spread its wings to dry. Another and another joined it, until five vultures held up their stiff black feathers like outstretched fingers, wings crooked at the elbows. They rotated slowly, each on its own branch. We held our breath. My son grabbed his camera, but the picture couldn't show how the warm wind lifted his hair from his neck, how whipped clouds piled up in the sky behind us, how he dropped to one knee to adjust the lens, how we were once again exactly the same height when he stood on the bottom porch step, or how, after a small mechanical click, one branch vibrated, suddenly empty.

Appendix to Volume 11

The movie of the past plays constantly in the head of the woman who can't forget, who is not me. She wrote it all down, too, volume by volume, gold numbers on the spines. I can't remember why. She never lost the house key she received. At fourteen, I rode by the surprise cloud of a wisteria in bloom, its thick brief smell of honey and laundry. Someone had checked the tire pressure and oiled my bike's chain. Someone else expected me. Later, a car parked under the streetlight by my window. That's all. The light was just light. Someone locked the garage and double-checked the lock while everyone else in our little house slept. A bottle broke against cement. Or laughter floated up as stars trembled like minutes on the face of the sky.

Acknowledgments

Tom, thank you for believing in my poems and the hours you spent reading and thinking about them. Kevin, thank you for creating the wonderful Press 53 and your remarkable energy and dedication. Thank you to my friends and family for good company. Thank you to my teachers for showing me what is possible. Thank you to my writing groups for encouragement, suggestions, and most of all, making a place to celebrate poems and words. Clare, thank you for mailing me chocolate and emailing the sweetest acceptances. Thank you to Nin for brilliant advice and reassuring second opinions. Margaret, thank you for top-notch proof-reading. Thank you to Caroline and Tony Grant and the Sustainable Arts Foundation for your vision and values, and especially for supporting my work. Rhys, thank you for feeding the bluebirds and hummingbirds and orioles, maintaining the ski boat, and making all my days radiant. My parents never suggested I might want to do something a little more practical with my life. Now that I'm a parent myself, I'm amazed at their generosity and restraint, and I wish I had thanked them while they were alive. I hope they somehow understood, and I hope they know how grateful I am now.

Cover artist Dawn Surratt studied art at the University of North Carolina at Greensboro as a recipient of the Spencer Love Scholarship in Fine Art. She has exhibited her work throughout the Southeast and currently works as a freelance designer and artist. Her work has been published internationally in magazines, on book covers, and in print media. She lives on the beautiful Kerr Lake in northern North Carolina with her husband, one demanding cat, and a crazy Pembroke Welsh Corgi.

Kathleen McGookey's prose poems and translations have appeared in many journals and anthologies, including *Best Microfiction 2019*, *Best Small Fictions 2019*, *Copper Nickel*, *Crazyhorse*, *Denver Quarterly*, *Epoch*, *Field*, *New Micro: Exceptionally Short Fiction*, *Ploughshares*, *Prairie Schooner*, *Quarterly West*, *Quiddity*, and *The Southern Review*. The author of four books of poetry and three chapbooks, she has also published *We'll See*, a book of translations of French poet Georges Godeau's prose poems. She has received grants from the Irving S. Gilmore Foundation, the Arts Fund of Kalamazoo County, the Sustainable Arts Foundation, and the French Ministry of Foreign Affairs. Her poems have appeared on both *Poetry Daily* and *Verse Daily* and been nominated for a Pushcart Prize. She has taught creative writing at Hope College, Interlochen Arts Academy, and Western Michigan University, and lives in Middleville, Michigan, with her family.

CPSIA information can be obtained
at www.ICGtesting.com
Printed in the USA
BVHW030013110620
581099BV00001B/90